COLLECTED POEMS

1937–1966

Martin Bell

Macmillan 1967

LONDON • MELBOURNE • TORONTO

St Martin's Press

NEW YORK

821
B434c

MACMILLAN AND COMPANY LIMITED
*Little Essex Street London WC*2
also Bombay Calcutta Madras Melbourne

THE MACMILLAN COMPANY OF CANADA LIMITED
70 *Bond Street Toronto* 2

ST MARTIN'S PRESS INC
175 *Fifth Avenue New York NY* 10010

Library of Congress catalog card no. 67–13754

PRINTED IN GREAT BRITAIN

FOR

M. A. B.

Contents

II

III

IV

Where move the enormous comics, drawn from
life . . .

W. H. AUDEN

. . . there are grounds for the belief that Fields
was dangerously bored by the time he was four.
From *W. C. Fields* by ROBERT LEWIS TAYLOR

To know that the balance does not quite rest,
That the mask is strange, however like.

WALLACE STEVENS

Acknowledgments

Acknowledgments are due to the editors of *Delta, Listen, Outposts, The Northern Review* (Belfast), *The Listener, The Times Literary Supplement, The New Statesman, The Observer,* and *The Guardian,* who have already printed some of these poems; to the B.B.C. Third Programme, which has broadcast others in *The Living Poet,* and *Poet's Voice;* to the publishers of *P.E.N. New Poems, The Guinness Book of Verse,* the *Poetry Book Society Supplement,* and the *Group Anthology;* and to Penguin Books for their kind permission to reprint fifteen poems from *Penguin Modern Poets III.*

My special thanks are due to the Arts Council of Great Britain, which made me its first Poetry Bursar.

A gothicised version of Nerval

Look for me in the shadow, a bereft one, disconsolate,
Prince of Aquitaine and heir to a ruined Folly.
One star was mine, gone out now: my starred lute
Goes in dark circuit with the Sun of Melancholy.

O, to console me, in my graveyard midnight,
Bring back Posillipo and Italy's seas,
The flower that was my sad heart's favourite
And friends the rose and vine there, binding trellises.

Am I Eros, then, or Apollo? Lusignan or Byron?
My brow burns red still, which the Queen has kissed.
I have lingered in caverns where the sea-nymphs quire,

And twice, a conqueror, swum the straits of Acheron,
Mingling alternate strains on Orpheus' lyre,
Sighs of the anchorite, wailing of the possessed.

                                              1944

A Benefit Night at the Opera

The chatter thins, lights dip, and dusty crimson
Curtains start dragging away. Then, at one bound,
A rush of trumpets, ringing brass and vermilion—
The frescoed nymphs sprawl in a sea of sound.

We give our best attention as we must, for
This music is fatal and must be heard.
The glittering fountains vocalize our lust,
The whole brilliant scene sways on to murder.

The idyll interrupted by a cough,
Coloratura soars into a fever.
After the vows, the sibyl shuffles off,
The conspirators' chorus mutter, melt away, leave us

A traitor and his stabbed tyrant, downstage in tears.
Masked revellers are grouping for a wedding.
In stern beat start to life six scarlet halberdiers,
Move with the music, march to a beheading.

Lo! Wild applause proclaims a happy ending.
Vendetta is achieved with clinking swords.
Sheer from the battlements the Diva is descending,
Rash in black velvet and resplendent chords.

1953

Usumcasane as Poet Maudit

Is it not brave to be a king, Techelles,
Usumcasane, and Theridamas?
Is it not passing brave to be a king
And ride in triumph through Persepolis?

Noses in books, odd children in good schools
Get praise by being clever. And they sing
Revenge on the fortunate, the easy-going fools;
And think it passing brave to be a king.

King then, but of words only. There's the rub.
Action is suspect and its end uncertain:
Stuck in a job, or browned off in a pub,
Or fêted and then stabbed, behind a Curtain . . .

Impatiently they strain their eyes
To see small faults through powerful lenses:
Angrily snatch at paradise,
Exacerbating their five senses.

Famous young Rimbaud managed rather better—
Crammed all he could beneath his greedy hide,
Went to Abyssinia, wouldn't write a letter:
Was made into a saint before he died.

The Enormous Comics

A Teacher to his Old School

Barnacled, in tattered pomp, go down
Still firing, battered admirals, still go down
With jutting jaw and tutting tooth and tongue,
Commanding order down cold corridors.

Superbly, O dyspeptic Hamlets,
Pause in the doorway, startle the Fourth Form
With rustlings of impatient inky cloaks—
Time and time again you go into your act.

Benevolent and shaven, county cricketers,
Heroes on fag-cards, lolling out of the frame,
Or smug and bun-faced, Happy Families,
Or swollen in shrill rage (Off With His Head!),

You lean huge areas into close-up
With cruel pampered lips like Edward G.
Robinson, or Tracy's anguished eyes,
And still remain the seediest of grandees.

Processioned hierarchically, larger than life,
Gigantic Guy Fawkes masks, great heads on stilts—
Your business was traditional, strictly articulated
Into timetables, only a few steps

From nightmare. Wild clowns will terrify
Wagging a wooden phallus at the crowd,
Raising a roar of response, of love and loathing—
Fat scapegoats stuck with broad rosettes of learning.

4

I listened and made myself little, still as a mouse
Watching the growling pussies at their antics—
Now I see, in the back row of any classroom,
Sharp impatient eyes, weighing me up for the
      drop.

Large masks creak. Sir will tear a passion to
      tatters.
One must pray for unobstructed moments,
For chances to be useful,
Like theirs, old wretches, like theirs.

Fiesta Mask

The raw feast rages in its fierce buffoons,
Flares in hot air. Calliope blares red.
Streamers, confetti, squeakers and fat balloons.
Here comes a great, big, daft, nid-nodding head—

A painted acre of face, a carnival grin,
With snouting nostrils, glistening carbuncles:
And children cringe, afraid to be sucked in
And eaten up by wickedest of uncles.

Once upon a time, some small boys found
In the next daylight's debris, after the revels
Had guttered down—the giant stretched on the ground,
Stupid in drunken sleep. The young devils

Began by throwing pebbles to sound the big head,
To find just what was under the disguise—
Started to claw the cardboard into shreds,
And one little bastard kept kicking at plaster eyes.

They battered at the craters he was breathing beer
    through,
Tore cheeks away in chunks. He didn't groan.
Soon there were ragged gaps enough to peer through.
And the squealing stopped. As if they'd been turned
    to stone.

RAILWAY PIECES

1 Poster for London Transport

Science-fiction, tattered and out-of-date
Bequeaths a landscape where our bodies move.
Flambeaux, portentous down the escalator,
Parade an avenue in *art nouveau*,
Herald a progress—Way for Captain Nemo!
Constricted corridors and halls of neuter wind—
How many years since they were tarted up—
Washed over in new styles of architecture
On top of Dali-Doré-picturesque?
Trough-of-the-wave-stuff now, in fashion's hell.

'Nor are we out of it', we mutter, pushed.
Official tormenters swarm, in diligent hats,
Clicking pedantic pincers. MIND THE GAP.
Lose the way and miss the underground connection,
All boredom condensed, fused to a helpless minute
Of pacing a grey slab at OXFORD CIRCUS
Between banked stares of glaring ikons—
Strenuous BEER and nubile CORSETS
AMPLEX GOD OVALTINE ELECTRIC RAZORS—
Only a stop away from TOTTENHAM COURT ROAD.

2 Hypochondriac Reading Newspaper

The sun-lit surface shrugs. An easy day . . .
No extra effort needed

7

To keep down monsters coiling underneath,
The hunched muscles writhing
In private hells, the gas-lit punishment cells.

Strained morning-face in the train
Keeps stoic lines, though careful to have ready
Accommodation, tolerant knowing eyes:
Only eager to relax, be safe a little,
Melt to a decent shape in smiles.

But always eyes find words to jerk fear back,
Something gross to be afraid of,
A thought to block the sun:
A twist in the dimensions
That can't be laughed away or worked away.

The ghosts are dwindled, only to re-form
More brassily efficient:
(Pale SYPHILIS deflated, pinked by penicillin—)
And see they all come back, infectious breaths,
Compulsive gripes to hold us gibbering

Bold CANCER, famous BOMB, blonde TELEVISION,
And statistical pressure of PUBLIC OPINION.

3 The Songs

Continuous, a medley of old pop numbers—
Our lives are like this. Three whistled bars
Are all it takes to catch us, defenceless
On a District Line platform, sullen to our jobs,
And the thing stays with us all day, still dapper, still Astaire,
Still fancy-free. We're dreaming while we work.

Be careful, keep afloat, the past is lapping your chin.
South Of the Border is sad boys in khaki
In 1939. And J'attendrai a transit camp,
Tents in the dirty sand. Don't go back to Sorrento.
Be brisk and face the day and set your feet
On the sunny side always, the sunny side of the street.

4 Southern Electric

After a week of fog, a mild bright winter morning.
Here I am in the train, reading Wordsworth to work
Without any impatience. Eyes stray from those pastures
And through the window find WANDSWORTH a peaceable
    beast enough,
Sprawling and arching a brick back in the sun.
And look again at the others, no longer lifeless
Waxwork heads nodding, fixed stares at newsprint:
Their eyes are mild with interest, wander without anxiety,
Without any impatience. The pressure is off.
There is no strain in the morning under the blue sky.
Have we ever doubted heaven? Why, already here . . .
At least, until we get to WATERLOO . . .

A Game of Royal Families

From the French of Jean Pervert

For Alan Brownjohn

First of all the King. Where's the King of Hearts?
The King is in his counting-house, of course.
And what is he doing, is he counting
His money up, just as one would expect?
No, he's eating tarts, a great plateful
Of jam-tarts, blood-coloured jam-tarts
Stolen to frame the Knave of Hearts.
(He'll have to look to his muttons, that one.)
Then the Queen, what's she up to? Where but in her parlour?
But not with the Knave of Hearts, oh no!
The Queen's mouth is sticky with honey only
When the Jack of Clubs roughs her up.
No need to ask about His Grace
Of Diamonds and His Grace of Spades—
In the linen closet, as usual,
Enjoying unnatural relations with each other.
But where's the swaggerer, Knave of Hearts, where's he?
Where would you think, he's in the garden
With the maid.
But that's no alibi, that won't save his head.
They'll get at her through her father, the hump-backed joker,
And she'll tell some story about a bird from the sky
Pecking her nose off.
But what this lot don't reckon on—
The people think her baby something special—
When he grows up there'll be a revolution—
Hurrah! Hurrah! Hurrah! Hurrah! Hurrah!

A Prodigal Son for Volpone

Conspicuous consumption? Why, Volpone
Would splash it around as if he could afford it,
Wore himself out for his craft, a genuine phoney,
Who only wanted, gloatingly, to hoard it.

His son had sprung like a mushroom, pale in an alley.
Reluctant, they had to unload the stuff on him.
To cook the accounts, got Mosca back from the galleys—
These lawyers worried that the heir looked dim.

What was he, now, to do with all this gold?
His father had withered in prison because of it.
Root of all evil, he'd always been told
By scholars who'd brought him up. Get shot of the lot of it.

Gloomy vaults, cram-full roof-high with piles
Of metal and stone and paper shoved into sacks:
A great city's sewer, bustling golden miles
Swollen for carnival. Must give it back,

Somehow get rid of it, be a big spender.
The tradesmen knew of a new purse spilling around.
Not a junk-shop in Venice that wasn't stripped of its splendour,
Not a period-piece, not an objet d'art to be found.

How richly the monde assembled at his parties,
How thickly clustered in slow gilded whirls!
Sensitive business-men and butch aesthetic hearties,
Senile young statesmen, faint expensive girls.

'Spend it faster?' He'd pay on the nail for their answers.
A patron's deep-waving harvest was quick to be seen.
A sculptor in barbed-wire, a corps of Bulgarian dancers,
Three liberal reviews and a poetry magazine.

Mosca's smirk broadened. The Foundation showed a profit.
How white and stammering now our Volponetto!
'G-give it to the city. S-see the poor get some of it.'
He vanished aboard a waiting vaporetto.

For one odd halfpenny, Mosca broke on the rack.
The Senate's liver was hardened with golden wine.
Some money drained to the poor. The young man never came
      back.
Last heard of, was herding swine, or turned to swine.

To Celebrate Eddie Cantor

The flesh is brittle, alas,
And ever-modish time, that fiend, is slee:
The Goldwyn Girls of Nineteen Thirty-Three
Also must go, must fade beyond nostalgia,
Vanish when celluloid crackles.

That year, not less constrained,
We strained the other way to find the future—
Eager and awkward, tried to look sixteen,
Be full initiates into the life of the time
And shuffle into the LYRIC, the local flea-pit.
We howled and whistled, fidgets on iron seats.

Our coming-in was brisk to music
Strident through raucous light along the slanting floor,
Underfoot rubbish and everywhere sweet disinfectant
Stinking like LADIES and GENTLEMEN—
The whole place blatant and blaring,
Usherettes sullen and louts obstreperous.

And, slumping back in seats, to see a flick,
Shadows to look at shadows, not expecting luck,
Amazed then, caught in your outrageous joy,
Dear Eddie!
                    Blank looming screen
And then you whirled from its imagined wings—
A small impassioned man who could hardly wait for his music,
A master, from Vaudeville, an accomplished master.

Voice soaring in gleeful lubricity,
Scandalous coloratura at full tilt!
Excited wide eyes rolling
And hands that have to clap that joy's too much.
Energy, wanton small bright ball
Leaping on top of the fountain—
Living water, extravagant
Flooding and cleansing the movie-house.

No endless exits down the sad perspectives,
The avenues of infinite regrets,
For you, Sir, No Siree!
Palmy Days, ample a blue sky
And the gross bull lulled to an euphoric calm,
Contented cows, O Don Sebastian—
The lineaments of gratified desire
Making whoopee with the whooping red-skins.

Thinly we rustled, ears of unripe corn—
You could have gathered us up in the palms of your hands.
Singing and dancing, you came out more than real,
Potent Revivalist, strong drink for shadows—
For you at the end of the picture
Bunches and baskets of flowers, all of them girls.

ODE TO GROUCHO

1 Invocation

Pindarick, a great gorblimey Ode
Soaring on buzzard wings, ornate,
Or tottering titanic on feet of clay,
It would have to be, to be adequate—
With the neo-gromboolian overtones
And the neo-classic gimmicks:
Pat gags cadenced from 'Mauberly'
In platinum-plated timing,
And tendrils convolvulating
To clutch the dirty cracks and hold the house up!

O flaking Palladian Palladium!
On a back-cloth rattled by oom-pah—
All our nostalgias, Hey there! the old vaudeville circuit.
Proscenium buttressed with brutal truths
Where sleek myths lean in manneristic attitudes,
Chalk-white in the chastest diction,
Sequined with glittering metaphysicality.
And massive ambiguities
Endlessly rocking a whole way of life.

2 Presence

What you had was a voice
To talk double-talk faster,
Twanging hypnotic

In an age of nagging voices—
And bold eyes to dart around
As you shambled supremely,
Muscular moth-eaten panther!

Black eyebrows, black cigar,
Black painted moustache—
A dark code of elegance
In an age of nagging moustaches—
To discomfit the coarse mayor,
Un-poise the suave headmaster,
Reduce all the old boys to muttering fury.

A hero for the young,
Blame if you wish the human situation—
Subversivest of con-men
In an age of ersatz heroes:
Be talkative and shabby and
Witty; bully the bourgeois;
Act the obvious phoney.

3 Apotheosis

Slickness imposed on a rough beast,
A slouching beast and hypochondriac.

Great Anarch! Totem of the lot,
All the shining rebels

(Prometheus, of course, and that old pauper
Refusing cake from Marie Antoinette,
And Baudelaire's fanatical toilette,

And Rimbaud, striding off to Africa,
And Auden, scrowling at a cigarette . . .)

Bliss was it etc. Smartish but fair enough.
We stammered out our rudenesses

O splendid and disreputable father!

Headmaster: Modern Style

For Philip Hobsbaum

I

This leader's lonely, all right! He sees to that.
Inspectors, governors, parents, boys and staff—
His human instruments—are all shocked back
From the stunned area round him, sound of his voice.
Wag, wag, of tongue is his wig and his weapon
Raking a stamping ground
For his mannikin's hard-headed strut in a neat grey suit,
For those liquorice allsorts, his barrow-boy eyes
(Shrewdness and suspicion go on and off like traffic-lights)
For the maggot-twitch at the end of his almost endless nose.

II

What a nuisance the little man is!
If two stay behind, to paint scenery
And he offers to help
They toss for who does the painting and who listens to him.

III

'Snitch', the boys call him, 'Snitch' or 'Conk'.
'Rats', he calls them, 'Slackers, Dirty Rats'.

IV

No Room for Gothic ghosts here
In the gleam of the public-urinal-type 1870 tiles—
There's a really up-to-date practical talking poltergeist
Resounds all day throughout the shameful building
That can't be prettied up, although they try:
It talks to the contractors' men on their small jobs—
He must slow them up.

V

And what does he talk about? Well, what was it?
Imagine a five act opera with only one voice,
Continuous recitativo secco monologue—
But in real life? And what is it all about?

It is for something and it isn't for you
It isn't something he'd want your opinion for
He's got it all worked out, he knows his line
Anecdote and anecdote and anecdote
To keep him talking, not to listen to you
Slugged into acquiescence by his knowing drone.

VI

He buzzes like pin-table-lights, flashing enormous scores
In disregard of what the ball is doing.
How does he keep it going?

Well, R.A.F. He was in the R.A.F.
A ground-staff commission in the R.A.F.
On heat with reminiscence on Battle-of-Britain day.
Knew how to get what they wanted, anything, any equipment
They knew their stuff, all right, when they occupied Germany
With nudges, winks, and Cockney chuckles.

And apparently spent all their time in the mess discussing
    religion.
That put him on to Christ. That's where your ethics comes
    from.
(He rehearses an operetta with a cane in his hand.)

Knows his way round any committee
Officials and contracts and regulations,
How to get round them, how to get praised for it.

VII

This poem goes on pattering just like he does.
This is the way to elicit expensive equipment.
The burgess are pleased to be stung for expensive equipment
(Quite a lot of the poor little wretches can't read)
New vistas in education, shining technical vistas

Showers and lathes and ropes and coats of paint
A new laboratory, new wood-work shop, new metal-work shop
Shelves in the library, elegant functional tombs
Where WILLIAM, BIGGLES, BUNTER rest in peace.

The boys should be grateful for all the equipment they're
      getting.

VIII

Let's turn aside
As Augustine might turn from a chapter on pride and
      concupiscence,
And consider poor Joe, Conk's deputy.

Joe does administration. It does for him. He's done by it.
Nothing comes right. He mutters about it.
Prometheus-Conk goes free. Joe gets the vultures.

Chief eunuch of the stock-room! Emperor of pen-nibs—
Footprints that vanish in the snow from Moscow!
And blotting-paper gone—to stuff the dykes?
The chalk they eat, the ink they drink. . . .

O the staff are a sore trial to poor old Joe!
They won't add their registers right. Their dinner-money's
      hopeless.
They will ask for stock on a Wednesday.
They send their classes down before the bell goes. . . .

Joe's tight face sits filling up the forms
And his small office shakes. A voice next door is sounding
About Christ and committees and polar exploration.

No doubt that Joe has still to be working, working, working.
And the Head to be talking, talking, talking.

IX

On Speech Day
The Chairman of the governors makes a speech.
An athlete makes a speech and gives out prizes.
The headmaster's speech is the longest.

Sea-shanties this year? No,
NON NOBIS DOMINE.

X

Let's finish this business off.
Let's take the backwardest class, 2 E say,
Up the last stairs, to the Art Room. . . .

They are so eager to do something
That they stop being awkward, knocking things over, sit still
    and attend.

Give out the clay. Never mind if they get it all over their
    clothes,
All over the desks, all over the floor.

'Right! Now I want you to make a headmaster.'

They will solemnly prod into life long-snitched headmaster-
    dolls.

Nothing crude like sticking pins?
Well all right, we will stick pins then, but also
Shove in chewed bubble-gum to make his eyes.

Give him a surplice of toffee-paper and hymn-book leaves.
Let bottle-tops stinking of yesterday's milk be gathered for
    his medals.

Ode to Himself

I

Go on, good monkey, make your bow, be me.
Appear as the polite one, the sensitive
Shy one, awkward but helpful,
Monkey of wisecracks, monkey who knows the words.

This social creature must ignore
All his disgraces, all the deplorable monkeys;
They antic behind his back as if they were at home:
Evil-tempered monkey with weak rage,
Envious idle incompetent monkey
A spiteful mimic of more handsome apes,
Belching wasteful monkey, timid
Monkey of tiny dishonesties.

Sad monkey, a self-pitying one,
Unlucky monkey, monkey who was framed
By mean streets in the shabby years—
Poor wretch of a monkey
In the freezing winds of time,
Almost a brass monkey.

Miniature snarling super-ego monkey
Squatting on the shoulder of the gross orang-outang

And stinking cynical monkey
Planning small satisfactions
In face of an abstract nothing—
What a nest of nasty negative monkeys!

II

Safer not postulate a central me
To be ambitious about all this
This chattering toyshopful of monkey puppets.
No puppet-master stoops
To curb their messy antics: monkey business
Must be endured
If only as talk in the head.

To watch is possible: therefore you must watch.
Sit down. Sit still. Eat your damned apple up.
The largest virtue is to pay attention,
Then watch intently, watcher in the dark—
Watch how a jangling piano-range of strings
Dangles a reigning Kong for every minute,
Wearing your shirt and tie, your beard, your spectacles,
Inflections of your voice and gestures of your hands,
Grimaces and grimaces and grimaces.

Old monkeys never die, fight back and never die.
They might fade away if you watch them.

And some already folding up their strings
Will lie down neatly in a cardboard box.
R.I.P. monkey. Then again, R.I.P. monkey.

New beasts keep crowding in the wings.
Here come the vulgarest clowns, red-cheeked baboons
With their pea-nuts and bananas.
Out-stare them. Staunchly watch.

III

The legends say the monkeys drift to sleep
Under clear scrutiny of evening sky,
Puff into cloud-shapes, fade away

And branches prick, impressive silhouette,
Pattern of monkey-puzzle tree.

Reasons for Refusal

Busy old lady, charitable tray
Of social emblems: poppies, people's blood—
I must refuse, make you flush pink
Perplexed by abrupt No-thank-you.
Yearly I keep up this small priggishness,
Would wince worse if I wore one.
Make me feel better, fetch a white feather, do.

Everyone has list of dead in war,
Regrets most of them, e.g.

Uncle Cyril; small boy in lace and velvet
With pushing sisters muscling all around him,
And lofty brothers, whiskers and stiff collars;
The youngest was the one who copped it.
My mother showed him to me,
Neat letters high up on the cenotaph
That wedding-caked it up above the park,
And shadowed birds on Isaac Watts' white shoulders.

And father's friends, like Sandy Vincent;
Brushed sandy hair, moustache, and staring eyes.
Kitchener claimed him, but the Southern Railway
Held back my father, made him guilty.
I hated the khaki photograph,
It left a patch on the wallpaper after I took it down.

Others I knew stick in the mind,
And Tony Lister often—
Eyes like holes in foolscap, suffered from piles,
Day after day went sick with constipation
Until they told him he could drive a truck—
Blown up with Second Troop in Greece:
We sang all night once when we were on guard.

And Ken Gee, our lance-corporal, Christian Scientist—
Everyone liked him, knew that he was good—
Had leg and arm blown off, then died.
Not all were good. Gross Corporal Rowlandson
Fell in the canal, the corrupt Sweet-water,
And rolled there like a log, drunk and drowned.
And I've always been glad of the death of Dick
      Benjamin,
A foxy urgent dainty ball-room dancer—
Found a new role in military necessity
As R.S.M. He waltzed out on parade
To make himself hated. Really hated, not an act.
He was a proper little porcelain sergeant-major—
The earliest bomb made smithereens:
Coincidence only, several have assured me.

In the school hall was pretty glass
Where prissy light shone through St George—
The highest holiest manhood, he!
And underneath were slain Old Boys
In tasteful lettering on whited slab—
And, each November, Ferdy the Headmaster
Reared himself squat and rolled his eyeballs upward,
Rolled the whole roll-call off an oily tongue,
Remorselessly from A to Z.

Of all the squirmers, Roger Frampton's lips
Most elegantly curled, showed most disgust.
He was a pattern of accomplishments,
And joined the Party first, and left it first,
At OCTU won a prize belt, most improbable,
Was desert-killed in '40, much too soon.

His name should burn right through that monument.

No poppy, thank you.

Dreams of Evasion

I

Deeper and deeper into softer moss
Like rolling downs, but swamp, electric-green
Velvetest counterpane but deeper in

Reeds pricking, sinuous knitting-needles, bunched
Further and deeper in to buzzing confusion
Where flowers eat burnished insects

Tufted sods sink, bristle, go soft
Stamp if you like, tread something flat
Shod feet will cut sharp shapes, but now

Footprints are filling vaguely with
Seeping, spread to shapes of bruises
Sucking is always starting under your feet

II

Water haze dazzles, spits on face
Flickering adders, threads of streams
Stitch, stitch, a brilliance, nets of spiteful talk
Incessant glitter and chatter, theft of soil

Zips gripping, streams bite, bite their way
Urgent to the river. There it lolls
A glint, through greasy banks. And nudges
It has eaten its contours into smiling curves

III

Must get away, must not get wet or dirty
Always a way out, always a bridge
Round the next bend, before the silver sewage
Dimples to whirlpools, piles to a weir
Be clever, find the fussy steps to reach a
Safe structure strutting, riveted in air

A saving thought commits, betrays
To muscles bulging twisted, sickening strides
Struggle for balance on the shining slopes
Of banks of slime
Straining to hold a distance from yourself
Blur lurching up, self in a mirror of mud

IV

On to the multipurpose bridge
Ambitious architecture vast hotel
Delicate metal blue-print convolution
Closet catwalk ingle oubliette
Ballrooms glaring jaded chandeliers
(Somebody's got to swing)
Bookwalled dens lined charts of Yarmouth say
And footman, footman, footman phoning columns
Frequent in alcoves
Tip the Vice-Chancellor something handsome
And pump the Padre's palm before you're topped
Climb, crawl, clamber, stroll or stride tiptoe
Polished corridors to priestholes
Stammer up mile-wide winding marble stairs
To bedroom, bedroom, bedroom, royal bedroom
(A good chap in a suit will arrange everything)
Avoid gymnastic apparatus, sides of ships
And small back rooms with private guillotines

Up and down in the lift from unmade bed to unmade bed
Through honeycombed conveniences slithered with shit

The ladder with the mathematic steps
(Ten seconds to solve each equation)
Leads to the gilt chairs of the Senate Chamber
Through a mouse-slit in the ceiling

One's scared to fall and does of course and
Screams right through the drop
                                        Falls
And hopes to wake up

Winter Coming On

A caricature from Laforgue

For Peter Porter

Fine feelings under blockade! Cargoes just in from
    Kamschatka!
Rain falling and falling and night falling
And how the wind howls . . .
Halloween, Christmas, New Year's Day
Sodden in drizzle—all my tall chimneys—
Industrial smoke through the rain!

No sitting down, all the park-benches are wet.
It's finished, I tell you, till next season.
Park-benches wet and all the leaves rust-eaten,
Horns and their echoes—dying, dying . . .

Rally of rain-clouds! Procession from the Channel—
You certainly spoiled our last free Sunday.

Drizzles:
And in wet woods the spiders' webs
Weigh down with rain-drops: and that's their lot.
O golden delegates from harvest festivals,
Broad suns from cattle-shows,
Where have they buried you?
This evening a sun lies, shagged, on top of the hill,
On a tramp's mattress, rags in the gorse—
A sun as white as a blob of spittle
On tap-room saw-dust, on a litter of yellow gorse,
Of yellow October gorse.
And the horns echo and call to him—
Come back! Won't you come back?

View halloo, Tally-ho . . . Gone away.
O oratorio chorus, when will you be done?
Carrying on like mad things . . .
And there he lies, like a torn-out gland on a neck,
Shivering, with no one by.
Tally-ho, then, and get on with it.
It's good old Winter coming, we know that.
By-passes empty, turnings on main roads
With no Red Riding Hood to be picked up.
Ruts from the wheels of last month's traffic—
Quixotic tram-lines to the rescue of
Cloud-patrols scurrying
Bullied by winds to transatlantic sheep-folds.
Get a move on, it's the well-known season coming, now.
And the wind last night, on top of its form,
Smashing suburban front-gardens—what a mess!
Disturbing my night's sleep with dreams of axes.

These branches, yesterday, had all their dead leaves—
Nothing but compost now, just lying about.
Dear leaves of various shapes and sizes
May a good breeze whirlpool you away
To lie on ponds, decorative,
To glow in the park-keeper's fire,
To stuff ambulance mattresses, comforts
For our soldiers overseas.

Time of year, time of year: the rust is eating,
The rust is gnawing long miles of ennui,
Telegraph-wires along main roads, deserted.

Horns, again horns . . . the echoes dying,
Dying . . .
Now changing key, going north

With the North Wind, Wagnerian,
Up to all those bloody skalds and Vikings . . .

Myself, I can't change key; too many echoes!
What beastly weather! Good-bye autumn, good-bye
  ripeness . . .
And here comes the rain with the diligence of an angel.
Good-bye harvest, good-bye baskets for nutting,
And Watteau picnics under the chestnut trees.
It's barrack-room coughing again,
The landlady's horrible herbal tea—
It's TB in the garden suburb,
All the sheer misery of satellite towns.

Wellingtons, long underwear, cash chemists, dreams,
Undrawn curtains over verandas, shores
Of the red-brick sea of roofs and chimney-pots,
Lamp-shades, tea and biscuits, all the picture papers—
You'll have to be my only loves!
(And known them, have you? ritual more portentous
Than the sad pianos tinkling through the dusk,
The registrar's returns of births and deaths,
In small type weekly in the press.)

No! It's the time of year, and this clown of a planet!
O please let the wind, let the high wind
Unknit the bed-socks Time is knitting herself!
Time of year, things tearing, time of year!
O let me every year, every year, just at this time
Join in the chorus, sound the right sour note.

The Ballad Singer at the Pardon of St Anne

From Corbière

I

Blessed the barren dunes,
Stark nude like the sea—
And the chapel of Anne-of-Palud
Is crude, too, and holy,

Of St Anne, the Good Gossip,
A granny for young Jesus
In rotting oak beneath a rich
Cope . . . richer than Croesus.

Beside her, the Virgin is small—
Fragile distaff, waiting for Angelus—
And St Joseph, upstaged, in his niche
Shoves his candle at us.

It's Her Pardon—fun and games and
Mystery—the stubble's hopping with fleas—
Anne, Sainted Ointment, cure-all
For mothers-in-law, and husband's ease.

From the parishes round about,
From Plougastel and Loc-Trudy,
They've arrived already, camping out
Three nights, three days, up till Monday.

Three days, three nights, the salt-marsh blares
With music—the rite's traditional—
Heavenly choir and singing drunks—
Beginneth the SACRED CANTICLE.

II

O Mother, carved out with a chopper
From oak heart, hard and good,
Your gold robe hides a solid Breton
Soul, all one piece, honest wood.

Green crone with a used-up face,
Boulder under the flood,
Fretted by tears of love,
Parched by tears of blood.

You, whose shrivelled breasts
Were plumped again, to carry
A purposeful virginity—
The Virgin Mary.

Proud housekeeper, mistress and servant,
Related to the Almighty,
The poor are pleased to talk to you
For you answer them politely.

A wand for the blind, and crutches
For cripples, arms for the new-born,
A mother for Madame your Daughter—
You've adopted all the forlorn.

Blossom of new maidenhead!
Fruit of wife's swollen udder!
Garden of rest for the widow!
District Nurse for the widower!

Joachim's Arch! O Ancestress!
Four-leaf clover! Mistletoe bough!
Medallion with a rubbed-out face!
Horeb! Jesse's Rod! Our way!

You kept the fire in
And went on with your knitting
As darkness came down round your lap
Where the Child was sitting.

You were there, the one who could cope,
Making garments in Bethlehem,
Still there, stitching the shroud,
Grief-stunned in Jerusalem.

Your face is a wrinkled map
Of crosses—your hair white as linen—
Keep from pedantic evil eyes
The cots of our grandchildren.

The born, the not-yet born,
Bring on, and keep them well,
And smuggle water from your tears
When God isn't looking, to Hell.

Take back little children
In white nightgowns, fading away,
And summon the old who are bored
To the everlasting Sunday.

O growl! The Virgin's Dragon!
Keep the crib safe and secure,
And keep bitching at Joseph
To sweep round the front door.

Pity the girl in the family way
And the small boy lost on the road—
If anyone throws a stone
Change it into bread.

Beacon on sea and on land,
Harbour, stars over heath,
Good Lady, through tempest, through war,
You beckon towards a good death.

Humble; no star at your feet—
Humble and strong to save—
Your veil in the clouds means peril,
Pale halo over the wave.

Those whose lives are a mess
—Begging pardon—sunk in the booze—
Show them the steeple and clock,
The road back to the house.

Fire the Christians hereabouts
With your own zeal, gentle and chaste,
And gather your simples, Wise Woman,
To soothe the horned beast.

Be an example to housewives
Of work and fecundity—
And say hullo to our relations
Already in eternity.

We'll line up an army of candles—
Spermaceti—the best—all the way
Round your chapel. We'll celebrate
Low mass at the break of day.

Keep our hearths safe
From spells and folk who are spiteful . . .
We'll give you at Easter
Flax, a whole distaff-full.

If our bodies stink on earth
Your grace is a bath for our good:
Shower on us in this graveyard
Your wholesome odour of sainthood.

Till next year, then. Here's your candle,
(Three half-crowns it's cost me).
Respects to Madame the Virgin,
Not forgetting the Holy Trinity.

III

And the faithful, in penitent nightshirts,
—St Anne, have pity, please—
Drag themselves round the church
Three times, on their knees.

And go on to drink the waters,
Miraculous now, from the hole
Where scabby Jobs have bathed . . .
Your faith has made you whole.

Down there they hold their suppers,
The wretched, Jesus's brethren,
And you won't see any miracles,
But real holes: Put your finger in . . .

On their hurdles they look like saints,
With scarlet nimbuses, each one
An owner of extensive sores
Like rubies glinting in the sun.

A barking man with rickets
Just can't stop his arm-stump's twitch—
Can't help elbowing the epileptic
Having a fit in the same ditch.

By a tree-trunk, mistletoe-bitten,
Stands a man with an ulcer that bites—
And a mother and daughter are dancing—
Choreography by St Vitus.

A father heats up a poultice
For a small son who's not thriving:
A boy owes a lot to his father—
The chancre earns their living.

There's an idiot since he was born,
An angel-blasted simpleton,
Ecstatic in his innocence—
The simple are close to heaven.

Watch, passer-by, all passes . . . but
The idiot's stare is stone and firm—
He must be in a state of grace,
For grace is outside time.

Among the crowd after evensong,
When the holy water's sprayed us,
A corpse sticks out, alive, a long
Leper . . . relic of the crusaders.

Then those who the kings of France
Used to cure with a touch—
Since France has cut off her kings,
Their God's cut his mercy by that much.

Put something into their bowls—
All our forefathers carried it,
The Fleur-de-Lys of King's Evil
Which these are chosen to inherit.

Miserere then for the junketings
Of these dirty old outcast Bretons . . .
But stumps can be managed like pincers
And crutches are weapons.

Venture among them, able-bodied,
But take care to keep your fleece on—
Beware of fingers that hook, of legs
Fixed in Kyrie Eleison.

And if you'd be sight-seeing, dear,
Take a look and turn back quick—
From under these scraps of rags
A scrap of flesh might prick.

They're hunting on their own estates
With Arms emblazoned on their skins!
Their hands have the droit de seigneur
Over anything clutched therein.

Offerings heaped—of rotting meat—
Heaven's elect—with death-house features—
They make themselves at home with God
For surely they're his creatures.

They're swarming in the churchyard—
As if the dead mistook the Day
Of Judgement, crawling out from stones
That crush the limbs they drag away.

We've no right to talk—they're sacred.
It's Adam's sin they're punished for.
The Almighty's finger has marked them,
The Almighty's right be praised therefore!

The scapegoats of the bellowing flock,
Loaded with every sin we're at,
God works his anger off on them!
The vicar of St Anne's is fat.

IV

But a palpitating note,
A gasping echo in the breeze,
Cuts across the grumbling drone
Of this walking purgatory.

Keening like a beast in pain,
She stands beside the Calvary,
Half a blind beggar, as it were,
No dog and only one eye.—

A weather-bitten ballad-singer,
Drop a halfpenny in her hat
And she'll do you Abaylar, Wandering Jew,
Or any other old favourite.

O but her song is long-drawn-out,
Complaining like a thing ill-used,
Like a long day with nothing to eat,
So lamentable her blues.

She sings just as she breathes, a bird
Without a nest, with no fine feathers,
Battering blindly as she flies
Round granite God, in granite weather.

She can talk, too, if that matters,
As far as she can see she thinks—
The main road keeps stretching before her—
If she gets hold of sixpence, she drinks.

A woman, oh dear yes—her skirt
Is strings held together by string:
Black teeth grip an empty pipe—
Life is full of excellent things!

Her name? Call her Misery.
Got herself born, somehow, somewhere—
Somewhere, someday will be found dead—
There'll be no fuss, no one will care.

If you come across her, poet,
Humping her army kit-bag—
Please recognize our sister,
Give her a few fills of shag.

You'll see on her furrowed face
A smile crack right across
Like splitting wood, her scaly hand
Make a genuine sign of the cross.

Blind Man's Cries

From Corbière

The eye is killed, not numb
A sharpened edge still splits
I'm nailed, but not in the tomb
My eye's got a nail in it
A cruel wedge still splits
An eye that's dead not numb

Deus Misericors
Have mercy on us
A hammer hits my head bang bang
It nailed the cross where Christ did hang
And have mercy upon us
Deus Misericors

Birds that tatter the dead
Stay away from my head
Dear God, you've forsaken me
Golgotha's still breaking me
Wait your time, black doves,
You'll get victual enough

Like a gun-port's hole my wounds
Burn red the whole way round
Like an old woman's gummy grin
Before she puts her false teeth in
Burning, all the way round
Like a gun-port's hole my wounds

Its circles of gold I see
A white sun eating me
Two holes pierced by a spit
Hell fire white-heated it
Rings and rings of gold I see
Fire from heaven devouring me

My marrow twists about
And a tear comes out
All paradise globed there I see
Out of my depths I cry to Thee
My brain-pan seethes about
A sulphur tear comes out

Happy the watch they keep
The good dead fast asleep
Blessed the martyrs chosen
With Jesus and the Virgin
Blissful the watch they keep
Judged, saved, and asleep

Stretched out under the skies
A tall knight lies
In the graveyard's holy ground
His granite sleep is sound
Lucky the stone man lies
With two untroubled eyes

You Breton heaths you stretch
Sallow around me yet
My fingers feel the rosary
And the bone Christ on the tree
Still like a beast I cry
To the dead Breton sky

Democracy

From Rimbaud

The colours on parade, dipping past the filthy bricks of this garrison town. Boots, newly issued, stutter on the cobbles; but we can keep step.

We'll be posted overseas, to the big Base Depots. White buildings in long straight lines, like the Big City itself, but with everything laid on, just for us. It'll be the biggest, best-run brothel in the world. If the students riot, it'll be us reservists who're called out.

East of Suez or thereabouts—where the cold beer is grateful to the clay that gurgles it up, and the temper rises nicely after meals. We'll make the black bastards work: leader-writers will talk about the Commonwealth.

Anywhere, to get away from home. Glad to be back in the army, we'll use our loaves, all right. We can't pass exams, but we get our feet under the table. Everyone else can get fucked. Progress we call it.

By—The—Right—Quick—MARCH

Instruction for my Godson

For William Redgrove

God help me, I'm supposed to see you're told
All about God the Father. So my beard mutters:
There are always two fathers, one Good and one Bad.
You can't miss the Bad One, he's always around,
Particularly first thing in the morning;
Scruffy and screaming for a razor-blade,
Wondering who to eat up for his breakfast—
He won't eat you however much he shouts.
I'm not trying to sell you bad old Nobadaddy—
Learn to shrug off his sessions on his throne
Farting thunderbolts and belching clouds.

The Good One has a different way with clouds; he watches.
He knows fifty-seven ways at least of looking at them,
He addresses them politely, and his looking
Can hold them still in the sky.

Letter to a Friend

Dear Russ, you're dead and dust. I didn't know.
I've heard it only at removes. For X
Who we detested, passed it on from Y,
For whom we had a jeering kind of fondness—
He read about it in the Old School Journal—
One way of keeping up.

'Organic disease' were the words. Which one?
Which painful monster had you when you died?
As good a life as me, I would have said—
You're one-up now, you smug old bastard:
'Christ, boy,' you say, 'I'm dead now.'
Stop dribbling bubbles of laughter round your pipe.

How many years since both of us owed letters?
Let's offer the usual excuses—
Marriage, of course, wives don't get on,
The housing-shortage, railway fares, etc.,
Weak putting-off, sheer bloody laziness.
We didn't want to say the way things went
Pissed on the hopes we entertained,
Naive, of course, but vivid and still pissed on—
The old gang born again in young careerists—
(Christ, boy, they're reading *The Times* now!)
As if we hadn't known all this before!

Gratitude, now, is what's appropriate.
How glad I am I've had your company!
After an adolescent's silly days
Of idle mornings, hypochondriac afternoons,
Thick skies that frowned and trees that swayed foreboding,
What evenings of relief have set me free!

Evenings of beer and talk, bezique, Tchaikovsky,
Hysterical evenings screeching at dull flicks,
And evenings when we gossiped into movement
The huge grotesques we knew, to keep us sane—
Hadji, Wokko, Nodger hardly knew themselves
And should we meet would start us off again.
'Christ, boy,' you say, 'Listen to this.'
Something new, I expect, about Taverner's sponges,
Drying, between the lying maps, in rows.
The sods today are duller and more utter,
But deadlier, deadlier still.

A formal ending I can't manage.
We've been solemn enough before, at Party meetings,
Constructive, eager, serious, ineffective . . .
'Yours fraternally,' then. And grin your inverted commas.
Help me to tell the truth and not feel dull.

High Street, Southampton

Mean enough now, re-built, street I once knew,
And tame and bright and tight and wide enough
Now, neat toy-town blocks of boxes, Noddy shops
With plastics wrapped in cellophane for sale.
A shiny hum of traffic with no pulse
Along the concrete now. Time to un-pin
Bravado, unfreeze tears, feel pain.

We missed the climax of excitement
In the old High Street, when it burned:
Twenty-two years led up to this, a loss.
Nineteen Eighteen, Armistice Day
Waves of excitement thundered round my pram,
The crowded skyline bristled in relief,
Shops packed in narrow cliffs rang joy.

But found no Ali Baba word to open
The caves to small boys' lust, each heaven cut off—
(A crimson wedge of steak, coffee to rape a nose,
Vast scented lilies, lobsters, brandy-balls,
Spectrum of ties from which to choose a week—)
The angel plate-glass scolded lack of means,
Banished a school-boy home—tea, homework, bed.

So Speech Day willed a jeering oil to blister
Forty distinguished Old Boys: the Mayor to be strung up.
Militant ARMS FOR SPAIN boards down the High Street,
And DAILY WORKER outside cinemas.
(A fat old bald man sighed, 'Ah! Propaganda!'

50

And livid neon smirked back from his brow.
And all the Fifty-Shilling Tailors' dummies sneered).

And after Munich put us into heat,
We went on talking, walking up and down,
A Saturday addiction, dear Unreal City!
And *enfin* Betjeman's slim volume came
To prove to us we loved, about to lose;
In small beer, posthumous, glowed wonted fires,
Rake's progress to armed forces of the crown.

Not there, then, in the blast, when flames were eating.
(My parents started walking out of town.)
Came back on leave, amazed, it was all gone,
Nothing was where it was and all was wrong,
And everywhere looked through to green of park,
Vistas to statues or to distant spires.
And scuttled, numb, to pubs still left.

Bar Gate survived, as usual, with its air
Of being left over from some other pageant,
Waiting to be relieved by Ham the Fifth.
Après la guerre, the G.I. saw a slum,
And wished himself in Naples or Berlin.
We met again and told old stories, hastily
Beat it for London, looked for jobs.

It's rough that there's no moral comes from this,
Only excuse for lack of roots.
Where is the Phoenix? Surely there was burning.
With more bravado still, some extra tears,
We just accentuate a usual gap.
Old stories for old friends, then shy away
And pick up, elsewhere, what we can.

Three Days

A pleasant way to finish the war off
At the convalescent Depot at Salerno,
Scrounging, on the Education Staff—
Run Quiz, Tombola, Brains' Trust in the N.A.A.F.I.,
Give left-wing lectures on the post-war world.
Plenty of cheap, good, spirits in the Sergeants' Mess,
And sea and time enough to swim off hangovers.

Armistice, Italy, was a fine, fine day.
We were awed and excited, suddenly free.
Finito Tedesci. Finito Boum Boum. And no fear now
To be sent up through squalid transit-camps
To front-line mountains, snow and mud and bang.
Sand the RED FLAG again, several times this time—
Alex had brought it off before Montgomery—
And a muscular Glaswegian R.S.M.
Thumped on the bar and glinted through black brows:
'It's victorry for the lads. I'm glad. I'm glad
It's victorry for the worrkers back at home.'
We left the mess and went swimming, drunk in the moonlight.

V.E. Day was a different matter, stale.
Started drinking in the morning, went on all day,
We'd expected this so long, and O.K. this was it,
We were rancid with expectation.
And Churchill wireless-spoke, fatigued. What was it?
Submarine bases, Ireland? What about demobilisation?
And a red-cap sergeant, who nobody trusted,
Lay groaning under a table: 'Four bleeding years!

Churchill! Four bastard years and a half!.
Churchill! etc., etc., etc.,'
True but tedious, we thought.

Next day got up with brass-sick mouth.
We went about our duties, sullenly.

V.J. Day I spent in Halifax, Yorks.,
Wilfrid Pickles' home-town, R.E. Depot.
They had the gall to get us on parade
For a major to tell us the war was over.
It wasn't we weren't pleased the new invention
Had finally finished things off. And no fear now etc.
But there wasn't much celebration, there wasn't much beer in
        the town,
And the locals wouldn't have a lot to do with us.
They'd had time to get used to soldiers, all through the war.

Bell's Elegy

The Bomb's been dropped again, in style, and how!
Fat clouds are worried over the debris.
A patch of blue sky stares. What happens now?
Angels weeping, of course. Mainly for me.

I

I said to Doctor Hackenbush
During abortive analysis,
'I hate the word, Love.'
I meant parents' unhelpful concern,
I meant they had to bring me up
To work hard and do without money
Just as they had:
I had to be neat and industrious
And flatter any bosses around
With my modest ability to cope.

II

My penis was dangerous, dangerous, dangerous,
Messy and dangerous,
In danger of being cut off.

(My God, the ducks were quacking for it,
And cocks ran round and round without their heads,
My grandmother's cat chased a rabbit's tail on a string.)

My bladder was sadder and madder and badder
When I used to wet the bed.
I remember a cold rubber sheet underneath.
(Dear waters, please, bring back the Flood).

My bowels were a sheer embarrassment,
Holding back in white-faced spite,
And then erupting generosity,
A richness on a social afternoon . . .

III

I didn't get very far, acting it out
With Doctor Hackenbush.
I developed, he said,
'A massive negative transference,'
So the analysis was cut off
After I hadn't paid him
For over two months—
He took two-fifths of my wages.
(His name wasn't Hackenbush anyway).
I still wanted to kill Stalin
After that. But I felt I'd let Freud down.
The cook would not run the State,
And the State wouldn't wither away,
And psycho-analysis
Was very expensive indeed:
Postpone, for the time being,
The New Jerusalem.

IV

So here I am, in the middle of several paths,
More or less where I've always been
Having survived war and intensive masturbation
Getting away with murder, maybe
But suffering Hell because I'm always overdrawn
At the bank whose manager hovers
Clacking revengeful shears.

Hey there! Nobodaddy!
That's *my* flaming sword . . .

Manicure

Each finger-nail, ugly again,
Must be clipped to a crisp moon.
Ten horny wedges,
A city's dirt under the edges,
Could sharpen to ten weapons,
Razors, flick-knives—mustn't happen.
An urbane law,
Not red in tooth and claw,
Says what nails are for:
Combing the eye-brows neatly,
Scratching the skin discreetly,
Squeezing black-heads, scraping corns from toes,
And picking one's nose.

Techniques for Détente

Que messieurs les assassins commencent . . .

1

Would have been pleased to help
Harvest the lamp-posts—

Each lean aristo's arrogant nose
Slowly describe circles,
And hard-boiled glares take in
New cycles, brash phenonema—

Each committeeing bourgeois
Feel rope through folds of fat
Neck—pressing up a grin
Around accountant mouth—

Once. But it's changed. Changed utterly.
We must love one another or die. A terrible
Beauty is born.
                    Jesus Christ, mates, I know
It's terrible. We'll have to put up with it.

2

Summing up and sending off to swing
Hardens facial muscle and
Sends nerves twittering,
Makes bowels plunge. Pass
The port. Tell me, My Lord, about it.

I share your nightmares, Sir—
Mr. Home Secretary.

I've got one, thanks, Mr. Pierrpoint.
But you have one with me
But let's agree it's disgusting.

3

I dreamed a heap of corpses.
They were vile and wicked.
I am an assassin.
I begin.

4

Thank God for the House of Lords
And the embassy to Outer Mongolia.

Let Bomber Harris
Enjoy his front garden.
Give him the first prize for lupins.

Let all the old men cultivate their gardens.
It's about time.

Let them wander up and down trim paths
Fantastically wreathed in sweet peas.

5

I nominate Mao
For the M.C.C.
He'll hit em for six.

I've taken up Mah Jong.

6

But the terrifying thing
Is houses,
A stake in the country.

One good down payment
And wages of a steady job—
A bloody-minded feudal lord is in,
In number fifty three.

Something to hand down.
Television performers
Become household serfs.
(I've seen suburban streets in Durban,
Nice people liking things nice.)

Dismal boxes voting tory.

A grip on the earth's crust—
Risky bravado.

7

Fellow citizens,
Forgive yourselves
Please. Forgive yourselves, please,
Thoroughly. Forgive your lack of status.
You'll never be impressive like new office blocks.

I break off here
To forgive myself a long and dismal list.

8

I forgive Stephen Spender.
I forgive Philip Toynbee.
I even forgive
Christopher Logue.

I award each simultaneously a Nobel Prize.

9

Why, Mr. Vxxxxxxx.,
How well you look.

Your holiday
Has done you good.

You must be full of beans.
The girls won't leave you alone.

(They'll shag him to death,
Them high yaller gals.)

10

How about it, Comrade K.?
What about Comrade Bukharin?

... And the big one you don't test?
Call it Lef Davidovitch.

11

I will sit down beside
The Earl Russell
To talk about D. H. Lawrence.

Poor sod, he's dead. Done down.

12

'Acts of injustice done
'Between the setting and the rising sun
'In history lie like bones, each one.'

Thus Auden, on F.6.

Well. Yes. Perhaps. However ...

Zen for William Empson

God nowadays spreads thinner than you think,
Is pretty relaxed, permits anything.
Stay quiet and at last you want to sing.
There's black and white and who knows which will stink?

We're all nut-cases now, and who kills whom?
Eichmann killed all the Jews by accident,
Killing goes with each historic event,
Hiroshima's bomb brought all the troops home.

We continue to work and eat, and keep
Begetting each other. Call it Society,
Years of doing things wrong. However

We all know we're near heaven when we sleep.
And learn discrimination by satiety?
Sign for *satori* on the never-never.

Grass, alas

Corn, actually, alas
                    stuck in their crops
Had to clean the grains out
                         with feeling fingers
After I'd lopped the heads
                         of these two pigeons
With kitchen scissors.
Had kept them hanging
                    three days as instructed
Over the kitchen sink.
                    I'd put paper bags round
To conceal
          the pretty pigeons hanging
From my two daughters
                    when they did the washing up.
Then I plucked them
                    plucked the small close feathers
From the plump fed breast.
                         I cut the wings off because
There was no point plucking
                         where there was no meat.
And then I drew them, that is
                         pulled their guts out
Through the arse-hole
                    (having got drunk before
This loss of virginity)
                    and managed not to
Burst the gall-bladder.

In the cooking
                I spread myself:
                    Salt, black pepper, garlic
                    Celery powder, bay leaves
                    Mixed herbs and tarragon
                    Two spoonfuls of red wine
                    An Oxo cube and water
                    Regulo 2, three hours
And sealed the corpses by frying
                                before I put them in the casserole.
They were all right.
                We ate them with
Enjoyment.
                Quite a lot of solid meat
On those small bones
                        but there was too much gravy
Too strongly flavoured
                    no good to keep it.
Cookery, cookery,
            quanto mi costi.

With Heads Uncovered

I'm glad I heard him speak
In a school-hall in Brentford

A few months before he died.
When he arrived the meeting came alive,

The candidate cut short his sensible words,
The party stalwarts cheered and stood and clapped and
    cheered.

He made a very good speech
Though only school-hall sized.

He twinkled and made little jokes.
He was plump and pink like Santa Claus.

He kept stopping for small coughs
And gaily complained of not being well

And his voice had a cutting edge
When he spoke of the DAILY EXPRESS.

(Among the journalists present one noticed
Mr. Muggeridge, a skull, grinning.)

But this was the miner's son,
One of London's best-dressed men,

Who employed George Orwell
To run TRIBUNE's arts-end.

One is reluctant to trust a politician.
Nye Bevan more than most perhaps.
He'll not be easily replaced alas.

David Guest

Well O.K., he was wrong
Getting killed in Spain
Like that. Wal Hannington
Sat and tried to argue him out of going.
He was wrong, he was wrong,
The angel has not descended, the state
Hasn't the faintest chance of withering away,
And nobody is sure which way Hegel is up any more.
He was the greatest hero I've met because he was brave,
And would argue with anybody,
And could interest people because he was interested—
If he was so bloody interested he should have gone on talking,
    gone on talking,
Something might have been talked out.
Near to a saint, he should not have got himself killed,
Thereby making himself an ineffectual angel, a moth.
The Professor of economics was right:
He just couldn't keep still at a public meeting,
He would keep turning round and standing up to see what was
    happening and who was talking,
And this was probably how the bullet got him in the trenches
    at Jarama.

Gabriel Péri

From Paul Éluard

A man is killed, he had no defences
But his arms welcoming life
A man is killed, he saw no other road
But one where rifles are detested
A man is killed and goes on fighting
Against death, giving up, forgetting

Everything he wanted
We wanted too
Still want it to-day
Simple happiness sun shining
Down on hearts and eyes
Simple justice on earth

There are words to go on living for
Innocent words like warmth loyalty
Love and justice. The word freedom
The word child the word gentleness
Flower names and fruit names
The word courage the word inventiveness
The words brother and comrade
And place names where we've been
Names of women names of friends
Let's add the name of Péri
Péri has died for what keeps us alive
Comrade, we'll say, his breast is full of holes
But thanks to him we know each other better
Comrades, we'll say to ourselves, his living hope

(Note: Gabriel Péri was foreign editor of *L'Humanité*, and was shot as
a hostage by the Nazis in 1941.)

Verdi at Eighty

1.

My brides are ravished away, are ravished away,
Two Leonoras, Gilda, Violetta,
One swaggering tenor has taken them,
One death seduced them to fever.

I have contrived a basso politics
To hunt him down, conspired
Through trio and quartette, strong situations,
Needled him on to my avenging sword.

2.

How shall a wicked, fat, old man be saved?
Connive with the women, incessant giggles and whispers.
He must be re-baptised in muddy water
And wash the district's dirty linen with him.
The wine will chirrup, an insect in old veins.
Ready then assume the sacrificial horns,
Grovel in terror before the Fairy Queen,
So that, our hope, lost lovers may re-join:
Nanetta find a tenor in the woods.
The festival will glow in basso nimbus of laughter.

Requiem for Norman Cameron

Becoming, for your death-bed, an R.C.,
Disposing neatly of N1, 2, 3,
One each to Heaven, Hell and Purgatory—
A thorough-going eccentricity
Imposed a pattern, stilled the flames
Raging outside and in and in between.

Still, lucky for us, your voice haunts
Under the hag, beneath the visiting moon.

Midsummer

It gets a bit wild
After three hot days
Even in England.
One is glad to see
Convolvulus
Get in there among
Pink civic roses . . .

Leonora

Small female cat, your tortoise-shell fur coat
Gently goes up and down now you're asleep.
The trouble you've cost us while you've been on heat,
Demanding to be let out at all hours,
Missing your morning liver,
To join the ruined choir of Toms outside.
Now you're asleep, relaxed and grubby,
Neat and detached.

I'll find your ping-pong ball before you wake,
Start advertising kittens for good homes.

White cats recline
on carpets, rich,
purring like Ispahan.
Carpets are manufactured
to advertise cats.

Get your cat to-
day. It doesn't
have to be white. It would
look well on any old rug.
A tabby is fine.

In Memoriam: J. B. Leishman

1

He was no good as a lecturer,
Droned through his notes.
As an appearance he counted, though—
Great beak of a Dante nose,
Coarse black Pre-Raphaelite bee-hive of hair,
Matthew Arnold side-whiskers,
And lumbering body mounted often
In ginger-checkered tweed plus-fours
On a district-nurse type bicycle.

It demanded a vast umbrella, black.

2

(His Rilke
Must have influenced
Auden's sonnets.

His was the first fame
I ever brushed against—
And nicest possibly.)

3

He held his Wednesday evenings
With a gramophone whose loudspeaker
Was broad and craggy as himself.
He would play whatever people asked for
(Somebody naïve would ask for
The overture to 'Barber of Seville'
Or else the après-midi of a faun—
And then some prig would bring in Bach.)

It was there I first heard
'Figaro', 'Così fan tutte', 'Zauberflöte'
'Falstaff', 'Otello'. And songs by Duparc.
He took care to provide libretti for everybody,
But for some reason didn't care for 'Don Giovanni'.

An early Glyndebourne attender—
I can only just imagine that clumsy body
Crammed into a dress-suit.

4

I asked him once
With undergraduate pertness
What had Coleridge achieved.

He replied by reciting
'Ode to Dejection'
In a basso voice that trembled.

5

He died by
Walking off an Alp.

6

Once his pipe was burning his tongue.
He made himself a hookah (narguilé, hubble-bubble)
From the two ends of it
And a chemistry flask and rubber tubing.

7

Three things I still copy—
His courteous use of 'Surely'—
'Well', to start an opinion asked for—
And maniac cackle of laughter, crescendo.

For Peter Redgrove

I

'It seems to me now a long time since
I was excited about anything.
I fill my insides with old man's bitter
And feel sour besides. How frail I feel.
And if I stammer now it's not young heat
Baffled, but an inefficient cricket
That never learned the use of its thin limbs
To make proper sounds. Fric, fric, hélas, fric, fric.'
Thus Don Senilio scribbled a climacteric.

II

A leisure morning sits him at his window
To watch grotesques outside. And he collects
An old man puffing, Sellars in a bit part,
An orange matron's parody of slacks.
Those children are too loud. And a great
Biscuit box of a lorry parks outside
And he can't see, puts gramophone records on.
A very old man might sit like this,
Remembering Dan Leno, Marie Lloyd.

III

Does he feel the victim of
Anyone in particular?
He has friends in offices, offices,
Less friends when they become
Dispensers of patronage.
Does he feel the victim of
The man who has adapted,

Become successful? Yes, he does.
Has he adapted? Not enough, at his age.

IV

Fatigued, fatigued is Don Senilio.
No longer can he summon elegance
To whisper, 'You too, valetudinarian'.
The clear and saffron *coucher de soleil*
Is lacking which could silhouette
Calligraphy of leaves in skeleton.
He shuffles at the bus-stop in the fog,
His feet begin to hurt, and he resents
The unattractive others in the queue.

V

Senilio's regime can not afford
Whipping by Venetian whores.
He has to suffer at cut prices.
Aches of decrepitude
Suffice him. Sweats and twinges,
Toothache, eyeache, hungover
Late haste to work, short breath,
Fear of the reaching crab.
He keeps spry, the old boy, considering.

VI

Senilio is stirred by curves of neatly
Trousered girls. But hair-styles bother him.
Mountainous, maybe, not, alas, of Bath.
Sometimes he thinks 'Rats' Nest', sometimes 'String'.
Sometimes, from tops of buses,
He awards marks for nubility
From a possible total of twenty
Instead of doing the crossword.
He regards the young with lechery and dislike.

VII

Sitting with bad companions in a stews
Senilio observed a veteran fall
Drunk in the fireplace. In stupid malice
He guessed, 'There goes poor Senilissimo.'
It was indeed that potent senior
Whose poems Senilio asked for as school prize,
And asks forgiveness of his gracious shade,
Envies his final slim volume.
Timor Mortis Conturbat Senilio.

VIII

The cigarettes are smoking Don Senilio.
He keeps on coughing.
The alcohol is drinking Don Senilio.
His memory's going.
He re-reads twenty pages of a novel
He knew he wasn't enjoying.
Paper piles up, piles up.
He has had to change to bi-focals,
Wakes at three every morning.

IX

It isn't work Senilio resents
But going to work,
Still having to go to work.
We're all slaves here and some are ageing.
It takes him longer fumbling coins for fare.
The old gentleman should be granted
Chauffeur, scottish rugs, silver flask:
He'd bear down on the zebra crossings,
Cackling as ushers scuttled.

X

Don Senilio
Tips the parking meter
A full half sovereign.
Outside the Turkish Baths
A constable salutes.
He's awarded the Prix Lamartine,
A Beethameer Fellowship,
And a Life Peerage.
Such seedy goods will keep him.

XI

It doesn't do to laugh at Don Senilio
Unless he laughs first.
He's in the business for laughs himself
And likes to calculate applause.
You musn't think him Doctor Bartolo.
He steals looks out of mirrors,
Adjusts veined cheeks, grey hairs,
And chooses a few words.
He'll time the laughs himself.

Senilio's Distraction Song

And patient monsters in the queue
(The world can't last. I am too mad)
Shuffle aboard the same bus too
Sit paired in seats, the sad and sad
I'd boil them down to the same glue
(The world won't last as I am mad).

Here's absinthe. You'd best booze it too
(The world can't last for I'm too mad)
Illumination could flash blue
To show what hopes are never had
And I might say a thing or two
(Before world ends. But I'm too mad).

Fair morning throws a milder hue
(Too late. Won't last. And I'm too mad)
On people looking decent too
But I'm not going to say I'm glad
Too late for me's too late for you
(And world must end now. I'm too mad.)

Senilio's Broadcast Script

Riposte to Peter Porter

Good evening. You know my voice. Instructions, now.
Section leaders will break open Cabinet P. *Cabinet P.*,
And distribute the jade-green capsules . . . Now . . .

Are you sitting comfortably? Then listen.
Here is music engineered
For this precise occasion. It will last
Eleven minutes nine point four three seconds.
Relax and listen with smiles, employing
Breathing rhythm Delta Ten One Three,
With, if possible, the modifications
In the last supplement. Now . . .

82

Repeat final cadence at end of poem

That's better isn't it? But listen again
O listeners sitting contented listen again
It's grave news now I'll pump into your shelters.
The end of the world
Has been postponed. (*Repeat and scream.*) HAS BEEN
POSTPONED.

Note: the music was specially composed by Anthony Burgess.

Senilio Re-reads Baudelaire

More reminiscences than if I was ninety . . .

Great ugly desk, each groaning drawer a year
Stuffed with bits of paper, crammed
With bills, bank statements, songsheets, tax demands,
Keepsakes for what, and letters never sent,
Scraps cut from the *New Statesman*, 1947:
My private secrets are more numerous—
The inside of my head's a catacomb,
Sad slaughterhouse, an Inca pyramid,
More corpses than Mortlake.

I'm a graveyard the moon hates as she shines on it,
Worms drag themselves all through and over it,
Eating and eating again my most dear dead.
I'm somebody's old drawing-room
Full of furniture about to become antique—
You could call it Betjemanesque—
There's a smell of lavender or lilies
-of-the-valley, is it? Anyway it smells.

There's nothing longer than the shortest day
Yearlong of frost and fog, traditional—
One doesn't want to know. The messy street
Extends a boredom to eternity—
Write off living. Come to life
At sunset only, down along the houses—
It's sunset. O.K. sunset, O.K. sunset . . .

Senilio Remembers his Grandfather

Wide pale pink grey-bristled bald-headed face
My father's father. He frightened me so much
I can hardly remember having seen him often.
His rages were terrible, his woman folk scuttled about
Except in his last illness, bloated bulk in bed:
My father used to shave him with a cut-throat razor.
He would suck his boiled sweets, then put them back in the jar,
Mean old sod. I blame him for
My father's keeping timid and respectable,
My aunts staying spinsters—
And only recently discovered what he did—
I'd vague ideas he went to sea but no,—
A gentleman's gentleman, sometimes a butler
Who drank. When he got hold of money he drank,
Was often sacked. My grandmother's wages kept them.
(I got all this out of my father, in his mild cups.)

Hail, drunken grand-dad! I like a thieving butler.
Your pale head looms leering out of your livery.
I saw an Officers' Mess cook once
Spit in a steak and kidney pie before he put the pastry on.

Senilio Passes, Singing

Solomon Grundy
Bored on Tuesday
Manic on Wednesday
Panic on Thursday
Drunk on Friday
Hung over Saturday
Slept all Sunday
Back to work Monday—
That's the life
For Solomon Grundy.

WORDS FOR SENILIO TO WORK INTO A PATTER-SONG

'*My body is a broad and blossoming meadow.*'
Vivian de Sola Pinto

I

My body is a relief map in eruption
Wrinkles wrinkles wrinkles riddle the landscape
Pimples keep on erecting and detumescing all the time
My face swells and subsides and always finishes older
I have one or two grey hairs among the hairs around my
      testicles
I give my eyeballs everyday marks for yellowness and
      bloodshotness
I blow my nose hard each morning to find out how deaf I am
My handkerchieves are filled with snot
When I make love I do it fiercely several nights in a row
As if it were the last time each time
Then go on the booze for a fortnight
Insulting my dear wife with silences

II

When I wake at four in the morning
There are always two landscapes inside
One is the mess one has made of one's human life
(I can say it only in dreams
I am always trapped in the leaking submarine, the
      executioner taps on the door
I am always back at school or in the army
Having lost my rifle not read Beowulf)
Two is the gurgling and splashing and undermining in the
      bowels
The snuffle in the bronchi and the sinuses
Orchestrating with bloody birds and aeroplanes outside
Cancer has captured this town and that town one says

III

One gets up makes tea
Discusses the possible public image with the shaving-mirror
Trims the beard sharp

One walks into the sunlight rehearsing wisecracks

One's wife will, mercifully, give one breakfast
Consents to gossip.

If Church spire be clëar
Twill be däamp round here

If it be not
Twill be bloody hot

When thee caän't see spire
Church be on fire

And we'll hang parson, squire
And the whole bleeding choir.

It is the Blight Man was Born For

I

Don't knock the door. She's not at home
To chat of Crabbe's or Cowper's verse—
Miss Austen's got the curse again,
This time, worse.

Strides over the moors
A recalcitrant Amazon—
Emily Brontë
With the jam-rags on.

Tears are replaced by
Crimson confetti—
Goblins get hold of
Christina Rossetti.

Poor girls,
I bleed for you.

II

Not given a classical treatment
By any English poet—
Not even Shakespeare.

Whose needling bloodied Duncan,
Sulks lost Actium,
Temper cast out Lear?

SENILIO AND THE MOON

I Running Mad

1

The moon is having her revenges
Inventing girls like the moon.

A sharp blade
Sails the sky.

I saw her through glass, through glass—
No cancelling that out.

What is it that I have
To repent of or relent?

2

I was stammering like a pundit.
At the back of the room appeared

A girl,
Clear and radiant,

Piercing. I glanced. Stammered again.
She went on shining, quietly.

II Senilio to Christine

'Ah! Ch-r-r-istine!'
Thus Louis Jouvet with his fine rolling of R's

In the film '*Carnet de Bal*'
Thirty years ago.
I was a boy when I say it,
And now I say to you, 'Ah, Christine!'

'Dans le vieux parc solitaire et glacé'—
Jouvet in the same film
Reciting Verlaine.
I would like to walk with you
In an old worn park
With fingers entwined

Chastely, nostalgically

III Double Sonnet to Somebody Else

1.	2.
If	It
you	would
were	not
Lady	need
Macbeth	any
I	additional
would	witches.
murder	The
Duncan,	Queen's
Banquo	crown
and	you
all	have
MacDuff's	already.
children	Bitch!

IV To the Same

Madamina:
You treated me like a dog.
Condemned to some machine
With whirring blades
Mincing to dog-meat. To be tinned.

It was true. I was cut into
Gobbets. How they flew!
But I'm back now, not tinned,
An old dog with
Intelligent eyes.

V Another Letter to the Moon

Your re-appearance
New as Laura
Restored my sanity

How refreshing a cup
Of water, cool friendship
And how flattering

With Primavera stockings
And a talent for verse.

VI P.S.: (Haiku)

Moon, I too
Can spell:
C, h, r, i, s, t, i, n, e . . .

Tradition's fine-meshed sieve will sift
Each man's re-gurgitated toad.
The thin pulse of the word must drift
Up the vague tides of Edgeware Road.

They jostle in the crowded room
Severely, not to be out-done
In rich Antipodean gloom
By Mrs. Porter's favourite son.

Below the ceiling, guardian of the Grail
The ghost of Dr. Leavis floats.
A trim breeze stirs the fragile sails
Of Lucie-Smith's expensive boats.

'Another spider!' groan the flies,
And stagger down the autumnal grove:
The honest gardener's mouse-bound eyes
Protest that he decays for love.

Poems condemned must lose their bowels:
Knit brows acclaim the execution—
Expressive consonants, rich vowels
By ladies trained in elocution.

A slow breeze stirs a beard Lear-sized
(Edward not King) to stringent rage:
'Not in the poem! It's not realized!
'An abstract statement on the page!'

1956

With a Presentation Copy of Verses

How nice to know Mr. MacBeth,
That Harlequin glinter and frisker!
What a gay air of 'I'm Colonel Death!'
Sets twitching each end of his whisker.

His appearance is feline and elegant.
He is certain of each fact he states.
His spectacles prove he's intelligent.
His degree is a good one (in Greats.)

May the verse-form remove my remarks
A little bit higher than platitude;
Though we're off after different Snarks,
Accept this book, George, with my gratitude.

Hemingway, Jimmy Bond, and D'Annunzio
Are not in my line and you know it—
You would surely have been Papal Nuncio
If you were not (hélas) a good poet.

May History's mischievous glass
Not show us out of our decades,
With me primly holding the pass,
And you at the barricades.

It Was a Violent Time

'. . . literary history; it is savage with gang-warfare.'
A. Alvarez

1

Who scarred the editor and smashed his snitch?
Which X-bard flashed a chiv, and which one wailed?

Who snapped whose umbrella, then
Tore down urinals, roaring?

Who told whose mistress, in waltz-time
He was out to get him?

Which megalomaniac said, aggrieved,
'You'rr the pushingest mon in poetrry to-day'?

Who needled whom
Into hurling a glass of water?

Who bashed up Pakistanis in the street?

2

Learn skills. Either the skill of a boxer
And afford to be firm and forgiving

Or deploy your sharp remarks
From a barricade of horn-rimmed spectacles—

That way you win your action for assault:
And when you stab, stab always in the back.

And pray for an unfailing hunch
To know which pundit to take out to lunch.

Jacket it winsomely in primrose yellow!
Here A, B, C are drained of words they said—
Decently wild now, each a handsome fellow,
With X, and Y, and charming little Z.

Footnote to Enright's 'Apocalypse'

Cultivated Signals types
During the campaign in Italy

Used to tune sets in
To German stations:

'The Nazis do Beethoven beautifully.'
And one American boasted

He'd caught 'Freischutz' complete—
Thus diminishing his boredom.

(Our chief culture–martyr
Was Glenn Miller.)

The Tedeschi certainly bought
Their magic bullets.

What have we bought?
What have we paid for?

Couples

Three couples in this bar, at different tables,
Two old, one young: the partners are like each other.
One has vegetable faces, chunky respectable
Carrot or parsnip faces: they look fed up,
Keep still, have company manners on:
In private this breaks down, one hopes, suspects,
In rootish laughter, wrinkled grins.
The second is restless and furtive and tatty,
Two mangey carnivores pacing one cage grey-pelted,
He fidgets pipe, taps chin, her fingers flutter
Round the gin she isn't drinking:
They talk and talk, unsatisfied.
The third couple is young, unworried, in good health—
Skin, hair, teeth gleam like advertisements—
They carry off their clothes as elegance—
Speak in a lively manner, gesture like film-stars—
For a few years now are priveleged, boss-class.

The girl, a bit plain beneath the glitter,
Glances round at the others,
Is troubled, briefly troubled,
Intelligent under her hair-do.

Anecdote

November afternoon, misty at half-past three,
Chrysanthemums still bright in slant of sun,
And two small girls chattering along the pavement.
The smaller said 'It was shepherds.' The larger, 'I know,'
'Praise him, praise him.' The other said 'No,
'It was shepherds.' At last it came to them
And they sang through a verse in wobbling unison:
> '*The king of love my shepherd is*
> '*And he that doth me feed . . .*'
Having accomplished this they shook off their Sunday School
    smugness,
And trotted away like little animals.

There was the mist getting close, getting closer.
There was the sun, an acid slant of yellow.
It had been warm and now was chill.
Most uncomfortable weather.

DIALOGUE

Corbière:

The song of self-praise goes on, too long, too long.
You'll have to sober up soon, old comrade,
And live an ordinary boring day through.
I died of TB at a foolishly early age—
Why do you have to act so finicking hypochondriac?

Bell:

You never had to live with so much praise
In pounds and shillings and pence.
They riddle my vitals, painfully.
It is not true that I am not in pain—
You damned unlucky *maudit* poet, you

And writing so well, blast you.

Ponge: Tree-Trunk

Since Winter's just about to put us on our mettle,
Let's show willing for the Wood's good offices.

Mad bells set off by less than nothing,
Outgoings at our expence, stop now, leaves
Whose whim can cover us or leave us stripped—
The trouble you cost to keep on imagining you
Already only just believable!

Unfasten, fall from me, too honest bark,
Fall to your mates at my feet, from other centuries,
Dead faces of dead masks, committee of husks
To accuse me of your fate, be witnesses—
All of them like you, moment-feeling skin
Which now we see by wet and soil undone.
You are my most intimate virtue,
But die as you must, in the usual way,
Die deliberately, debunk unhappy fate.

And thus the tree is quick beneath its bark
Sharpening the profile death will make perfect.

Whistling a Sober Little Tune: Sunday Lunch-Time

For Edward Lucie-Smith

GOD IS this
very tiny insect moving
automatic as it were and clockwork slowly
over Hart Crane's page.
Would I have noticed IT
on, say, 'The Sunday Times'
which hasn't these wide margins?
I would like to care for IT
but what can one do for an insect?

Practical help is practical only
where appropriate.
Try without hysteria to avoid if
possible killing IT,
except when one is sure IT is a killer.

Pensées for Blaise

1
God is
    a deep breath
    a vote of confidence
    a final stoic gesture

One must be awake in Nirvana
    or its no good.

2
Marx would not have said
    religion
    is the opium of the people
Unless
    he was desperate for something like opium.

3
I lack D. H. Lawrence's
    desperate belief
    in his own vitality

It killed him in the end too.

4
Of all the religious temperaments
I find Hart Crane the most sympathetic
But do not intend to drown myself
Even in drink.

5

I'm still alone
>   after writing all this:
>   God hasn't spoken,

alone and frightened
>   I will find some distraction.

6

Je vais me raser
>   and put on a tie, turn
>   the corners of my mouth down
>   like Charles.

Pride, devilish pride.

Axioms

For Titus Oates

1

The brain sharpens its politics.
The personality falls apart.

2

'Good' and 'Will.'
When I will good I am willing my will.

3

Power is plaudits
And various sleazy appurtenances.

4

I won't try to persuade these people.
They would end by liking me.

5

I don't like these people.
They would cheapen my ideas.

PETS

For Anthony and Lyn Burgess

1

Domestication for use
At first. Took time,
Could be difficult.
'A good man with animals'
Still commands a price
Like a good garage mechanic.

Provided fleece
Fattened for slaughter
Provided milk
Fattened for slaughter
Provided transport
Fattened for slaughter

Provided meat, provided meat
Red steak, brown crackling

And some hunted others
Foxes, rats, mice, and such small deer
Got the run of the house

Some castrated
Some kept for breeding
Some fed in winter
Inside the hut for warmth

2

Fetiches elegant profiles
On cave walls
Worshipped killed eaten
Before suburban brick spread

Tamed totems in flats and gardens
Pussies and bow-wows
Mabel Lucie Atwill
Georgian poets

The idea of the sacred
Has lost class—
A castrated one
Plump and decorative

Writhing on a gate-post.
Fierceness one can fumble.

3

My four kittens are being cute on the carpet
They know where their piss-box is, they'd better

I could have drowned the lot
Before their mother's triumphant birth-purr was finished

I could seize a kitten
Dash out its brains on the tiles

I can get them
Neutered or spaded

But I pick them up, stroke them
Play with them like babies

They play with each other
Stalk scratch bite

I let them climb all over me.
I hope I can give them away.

    4
Most of my cats
Came to unlucky ends.

Pinto, made silly by air-raids
Had to be put down.

Jezebel was put down too.
The landlord wouldn't stand kittens.
I hope her descendants are still about
Being a nuisance.
I still feel sick about it.

Heroic Rochester, lean tom
Could leap through inches at the top of the window—
Dragged to the edge of the house and died
With his red guts hanging out.
Three days later we found him, after
Calling 'Rochester, Rochester, Rochester.'
I could kill whoever killed him.

    5
One identifies and feels
A general sense of doom,
Bombs and lung cancer.
(I hope I can give them away to good homes.)

A nuisance all over every room,
'An object for children to learn benevolence from.'
One watches where one puts one's foot.

At present my manners are
                              wreathing and leaping and
Purring for raw liver.

Unfriendly Flowers

Startled, the gardener learns to fear his art—
Seeing spring up, after long, loving hours
Of labour in the garden of his heart,
The vivid, the metallic the unfriendly flowers.

1937

My Blue Heaven

Light hitting you in the eye
Like Sorbo bounced from the asphalt
Light from the pale-blue plaster sky
Light from the glitter of the blue water
Flapping full on the shore.

Of course there are paler-trees dotted about all over
the place.

The streets are full of friendly faces
And trains dash in and out of the station all day long.

1938

Lecture Notes

let us pass on
    to consider the influence of Anglo-Norman
    to insist that angels and policemen wear black shirts
    jump through the window jump out of the door
    to say, quite suddenly and risen from the dead
    'I, I am Popeye, the Sailor Man'

let us pass on, O, let us pass on
    to the liquidation of Narcissus
    to the decapitation of Father Christmas
    to the final boiling of glass eyes

                               1937

Prospect 1939

For Campbell Matthews

'Life is a journey' said our education,
And so we packed, although we found it slow.
At twenty-one, left stranded at the station
We've heaps of luggage and nowhere to go.

PRINTED IN GREAT BRITAIN BY ROBERT MACLEHOSE AND CO. LTD
THE UNIVERSITY PRESS, GLASGOW